AN ALL-NATURAL PLANT FOOD,
YEAST

is a treasure-trove of vitamins, minerals and body-building proteins. The value of yeast as a Nature-created food has become more and more widely recognized as the search for better health and natural cookery has grown.

Because it is a plant food, easily available and very inexpensive, it is especially welcomed by those who seek a meatless source of top-quality nutrients.

Yeast flakes are flavorful, tasty and deliciously good when added to any kind of food, cooked or raw.

And here is the book that tells you when, how much, and how to add health to your diet—taste to your food—and saved money to your budget!

THE
YEAST FLAKES
COOKBOOK

CARLSON WADE

A JOVE BOOK

THE YEAST FLAKES COOKBOOK

A Jove Book / published by arrangement with
the author

PRINTING HISTORY
Pyramid edition / March 1973
Second Pyramid printing / April 1977
Jove edition / July 1982
Second printing / September 1982

ISBN: 0-515-02904-1

Jove books are published by Jove Publications, Inc.,
200 Madison Avenue, New York, N.Y. 10016. The words
''A JOVE BOOK'' and the ''J'' with sunburst are trademarks
belonging to Jove Publications, Inc.

PRINTED IN THE UNITED STATES OF AMERICA

THE
YEAST FLAKES
COOKBOOK

TABLE OF CONTENTS

INTRODUCTION

Yeast is an all-natural plant food that is a treasure trove of vitamins, minerals and body-building proteins. The value of yeast as a Nature-created food has become more and more widely recognized as the search for better health and natural cookery has grown. It is often hailed as a "wonder food" brimming with almost "Fountain of Youth" nutrients that work to build and rebuild the body—and the mind. Because it is a plant food, it is especially welcomed by those who seek a meatless source of top-quality nutrients. Yeast is flavorful, tasty and deliciously good when added to almost any kind of food, cooked or raw.

The Yeast Flakes Cookbook is a collection of kitchen-tested recipes using yeast as an ingredient. It will enable you to transform an ordinary, simple dish into a masterpiece of gustatory pleasure with the addition of a small amount of the substance. The recipes show you how to add a mouth-watering taste to such common foods as breads, rolls, meat, fish, poultry, eggs, dairy products, fruit and vegetable salads, soups, sauces and dressings, desserts. Just a small amount of yeast can create a magnificent culinary delight.

The Yeast Flakes Cookbook will help you feast on yeast! The most humble of foods take on an edge of exotic delight and feast-like delicious goodness that will win you praises as a cook . . . and tummy-pleasing pleasure and body-building nutrients as well.

All these recipes have been carefully created to provide a goodly supply of health-improving nutrients. The combination of good taste and good nutrition helps make this book a bonanza of healthy cooking!

To derive maximum benefit and enjoyment from this cookbook, use all-natural and organically grown ingredients. These are available at health food stores and even many large supermarkets.

The Yeast Flakes Cookbook will help you achieve the glow of good health via the pleasures of good cooking with natural products. We hope it is the start of an adventure in your quest for the joy of good health.

Good taste and good health to all!

CARLSON WADE

10

CHAPTER 1

INTRODUCING YEAST FLAKES

"Brewer's yeast" is a phrase that is taken from the days when dry and debittered yeast was a brewer's industry byproduct. Today, we call the same substance "yeast flakes" or "nutritional yeast."

YEAST—WHAT IS IT? Yeast is an all-natural plant product which has been grown solely for food. It is the smallest of all cultivated plants—about 1/4000th of an inch in diameter, or about the size of a human blood corpuscle. The tiny yeast plant is grown on a food substance called "wort," an herbaceous plant root. Often, cereal grains and hops (twining vines of the mulberry plant family) are added to further nourish the yeast plant and help it become naturally enriched with tasty nutrients.

HOW YEAST IS GROWN. The yeast plant is placed in large vats until it has produced the maximum amount of yeast cells possible. The seed bed is cultivated under carefully controlled temperatures. Growth and harvest of the yeast plants are supervised in much the same way that agriculturists guide the production of fruits and vegetables. All this is done so that top-quality plants will be the result, plants brimming with vitamins, minerals and proteins.

HOW YEAST IS HARVESTED. Once the yeast plant has grown to peak form, which is carefully determined, it is then harvested. It is washed and dried in an all-natural way that preserves all of the rich nutrients. It is prepared then just as carefully, for the same reasons, and emerges in the form of edible yeast flakes.

THE VALUE OF YEAST. The microscopic yeast plant has the ability to reproduce at an amazingly fast rate in a process called "budding." This reproductive process creates a rich naturally available supply of vitamins, minerals and proteins. Yeast is a much-desired and highly economical food, too, when compared to other nutritious products such as meat, eggs, dairy products. Allowed to multiply and store up its own self-created "health bombs," it stands alone as an inexpensive source of highly valuable nutrients.

THE NUTRITIONAL GOODNESS OF YEAST. Yeast flakes are far and away our most economical sources of the B-complex vitamins, minerals and protein. It may take months to grow soybeans, sunflower seeds, peanuts; it takes years to grow dairy cattle and beef; but it takes only a few hours to grow yeast. Being a plant food, it is doubly desirable by those who are seeking a meatless source of healthful elements.

Yeast has all the elements of the B-complex vitamin family. It has 16 of the 20 amino acids (forms of protein that are essential for the proper functioning of our bodies, for longevity, for resistance to disease, for rebuilding the tissues that illness has weakened), and some 18 minerals. Since the body needs some 60 nutrients daily, it is obvious that food yeast makes most of them easily available. Furthermore, yeast flakes will offer more of them than any other single food, with the exception of liver.

NUTRITIVE VALUES OF YEAST FLAKES

(Values are calculated on the measurement of 100 grams of yeast flakes, or ¼ cup.)

Key Nutrient	Potency	What It Does
Water	7.0 grams	Helps carry nutrients to cells and wash waste products away, regulates temperature, aids digestion, builds tissues.
Vitamin B₁ (Thiamine)	9.69 milligrams	Necessary for the body's proper use of carbohydrates. Acts as a helper (coenzyme) in important energy-yielding reactions in the body.
Vitamin B₂ (Riboflavin)	5.45 milligrams	Necessary for healthy skin. Helps prevent sensitivity of the eyes to light. Essential for building and maintaining body tissues

13

Key Nutrient	Potency	What It Does
		and the use of oxygen by cells.
Vitamin B₃ (Niacin)	36.2 milligrams	Necessary for converting food to energy, acting in many energy-yielding reactions. Aids in soothing nervous system.
Protein	36.9 grams	Builds and repairs all tissues. Helps build blood and form antibodies to fight infection. Supplies energy.
Fat	1.6 grams	Supplies large amount of energy; aids in transport of other nutrients. Essential fatty acids help maintain good health.
Carbohydrates	37.4 grams	Supplies energy, regulates blood sugar, carries other nutrients present in foods to most body parts.
Calcium	106 milligrams	Helps build bones and teeth; helps blood clot; helps muscles and nerves function and regulates the use of other body minerals.
Phosphorus	1893 milligrams	Helps internal growth, repair; aids bloodstream in neutralizing excess acid and maintaining a healthy alkaline balance. Enzyme activator, helps in digestive processes.

Key Nutrient	Potency	What It Does
Iron	18.2 milligrams	Provides oxygen to billions of body tissues and muscle cells. A vital component of hemoglobin, nourishes red blood cells.
Sodium	150 milligrams	*Natural* sodium helps control osmotic pressure and fluid passage between tissues and blood. Helps muscle contract and improves nerve impulses.
Potassium	1700 milligrams	Controls body fluids, normalizes heartbeat, nourishes muscles, keeps kidneys healthy, casts off waste products.

OTHER NUTRIENTS IN YEAST FLAKES. Other valuable nutrients in yeast flakes include Vitamin B₆ (pyridoxine), Vitamin B₁₂, folic acid, pantothenic acid, biotin; all work together with many of the minerals and amino acids to create a healthy source of good nutrition.

HEALTH BUILDING POWER IN ONE TABLESPOON OF YEAST FLAKES. Just one tablespoon of yeast flakes will offer these health-building power benefits: 4.6 grams of protein, .2 grams of essential fatty acids, 3.7 grams carbohydrates, 11 milligrams of calcium, 189 milligrams of phosphorus, 1.8 milligrams of iron, 1.2 milligrams of thiamine, .54 milligrams of riboflavin, 3.6 milligrams of niacin.

SPECIAL BONUS: One tablespoon of yeast flakes has:

As much protein as ¼ cup of wheat germ.

As much calcium as ½ cup of orange juice.

As much phosphorus as ¼ pound of fillet of haddock.

As much iron as 1 cup of cooked spinach.

As much thiamine as 1 cup of wheat germ.

As much riboflavin as 4 eggs.

As much niacin as ½ cup brown rice.

Yes, all this and much, much more in healthfully good, natural and meatless yeast flakes—Nature's treasure of delicious nutrition.

CHAPTER 2

THE EASY WAY
TO USE YEAST FLAKES
IN EVERYDAY COOKING

To begin, how much of yeast flakes should you take daily? This depends upon your personal preferences and needs. But with so much widespread nutritional deficiency, a regular daily intake is often a wise course to follow.

OFFICIAL RECOMMENDATION. *The United States Dispensatory* is the official book describing and defining drugs and medicines. It sets forth official standards that are guidelines for physicians.

This official source recommends a 10-gram dose, four times daily. One tablespoon equals 10 grams; therefore, if you take four tablespoons daily, you will be taking the amount recommended by this official source. You may wish to increase this amount if you feel you want to have optimum good health.

Since each person is different, the most beneficial amount will vary.

HOW TO BEGIN TAKING YEAST FLAKES. Because the yeast flakes have a concentrated taste, you should begin taking this food in smaller quantities until it becomes familiar and finally highly palatable to your taste buds. Begin with one-half teaspoonful daily. Gradually, increase to one full teaspoonful daily. Once you are used to the taste, and if you wish, you may take several tablespoonfuls daily.

HOW TO USE YEAST FLAKES. Here are several suggestions:

Yeast Beverage: The United States Dispensatory suggests that you mix a small amount of the flakes with milk, fruit or vegetable juices, soup or other hot beverage. Rub to a paste with a *small amount* of the liquid; then mix with the larger amount. Stir vigorously, and then drink slowly.

Yeast Health Tonic: In a pint of raw fruit or vegetable juice, add 4 tablespoons of yeast flakes. Stir vigorously. Set in your refrigerator. The lumps will dissolve on standing. When ready to use, stir well and pour into a glass. TIP: Have a pint of this yeast health tonic always ready for use to enjoy throughout the day as a healthy thirst-quencher.

Yeast-'n'-Milk: Beat together these ingredients: 1 to 2 cups of fresh skim milk, ½ cup powdered skim milk, 1 to 4 heaping tablespoons of yeast flakes, 1 to 3 teaspoons blackstrap molasses. Beat or blend *smooth.* Add some more fresh milk, if desired. Drink one to two glasses of Yeast-'n'-Milk daily for a concentrated dose of the valuable vitamins, minerals, proteins, enzymes, needed for good health.

Baked Foods: Add yeast flakes to almost all baked goods, such as breads, rolls, muffins, biscuits, pancakes, buns. Just add desired amount to the batter and keep kneading or stirring until the flakes are thoroughly blended, and bake as usual.

Main Dishes: Sprinkle desired amount of yeast flakes to such main dishes as stews, casseroles, goulash, meat loaf, poultry, fish, dairy dishes. TIP: Yeast flakes blend beautifully with foods that have strong flavors themselves, as well as with strong spices and herbs.

Sandwiches: Mix small amounts of yeast flakes into peanut butter, natural jams or jellies, in chopped egg, fish, vegetable or meat salads that are used as sandwich spreads. It creates a piquant flavor, boosting the taste appeal as well as the healthiness of the sandwich.

Extra Tips: Sprinkle yeast flakes in hot soups; stir vigorously before serving. Sprinkle yeast in salad dressings, in all kinds of sauces. Sprinkle yeast flakes over fruit salads as well as other vegetable salads, mix the yeast flakes with the salad dressing to create a thrilling taste treat chock full of good nutrition. Yeast flakes may also be sprinkled in yogurt that has been mixed with whole wheat germ flakes for a luscious luncheon-in-a-cup.

The purpose of the *Yeast Flakes Cookbook* is to introduce you to the exciting adventure of gourmet eating with this healthful food. The recipes that follow all contain yeast flakes. Just add a small quantity of this food and simple fare is transformed

19

into a mighty mountain of great eating and grand nutrition.

DON'T FORGET: Every grain of yeast is *food*. Good food. All food. No waste. A complete food in itself, from Nature to your plate.

Yeast flakes may truly become the newly discovered "missing link" in your quest for good health and good eating.

CHAPTER 3

BEVERAGES—HOT AND COLD

HOLLYWOOD BREAKFAST CUP

¾ cup milk
½ cup fruit juice
1 egg
1 teaspoon honey
2 tablespoons raw wheat germ
¼ teaspoon yeast flakes

Measure all ingredients into a small bowl or blender jar. Blend at high speed or use a rotary beater, until thoroughly mixed. Serve comfortably cold. Serves 1.

MORNING YEAST SHAKE

¾ cup milk
⅓ cup tomato juice
2 tablespoons wheat germ
½ teaspoon yeast flakes

Measure all items into a small bowl or blender jar.
Blend at high speed with blender, rotary beater or
mixer, until thoroughly mixed. Serve comfortably
cold. Serves 1.

SOOTHING NIGHTCAP

¾ cup skimmed milk
¼ cup desired fruit sherbet
1 tablespoon wheat germ
1 teaspoon yeast flakes

Measure all ingredients into a small bowl or blender jar. Blend at high speed with blender, rotary
beater or mixer, until thoroughly mixed. Serve comfortably cold. Serves 1.

NO-COFFEE COOLER

½ teaspoon yeast flakes
2 cups cold milk
⅛ teaspoon vanilla
1 egg
1 tablespoon wheat germ
1 teaspoon honey
2 teaspoons Postum or coffee substitute

Measure all ingredients into a small bowl or blender
jar. Blend at high speed with blender, rotary beater

or mixer, until thoroughly mixed. Serve comfortably cold. Serves 1.

HOT MULLED APPLE NOG

1½ cups boiling water
¼ cup honey
½ lemon, sliced
3 sticks cinnamon
3 whole cloves
1 tablespoon yeast flakes
1 quart apple juice

Combine boiling water, honey, lemon, cinnamon, cloves, yeast flakes; stir until thoroughly blended. Now add apple juice; simmer 20 minutes. *(Do not boil!)* Strain. Serve hot with a sprinkling of nutmeg. Serves 4-6.

`HOT LEMON SWIZZLE EGGNOG

1 quart commercial eggnog
1 cup milk
1 cup fruit juice
¼ teaspoon salt substitute
2 teaspoons grated lemon rind
1 teaspoon yeast flakes
Nutmeg
Curls of lemon peel

Combine eggnog and milk. Slowly beat in fruit juice. Stir in salt substitute, lemon rind and yeast flakes. Heat gently to just below boiling. Top each serving with a dash of nutmeg and a lemon peel curl. Serves 4-6.

HOT CRANBERRY CUP

1 quart cranberry juice
2 cups water
½ cup honey
4-inch cinnamon stick
12 whole cloves
Peel of ½ lemon
2 glasses fresh fruit juice
1 tablespoon yeast flakes
¼ cup lemon juice
Nutmeg

Combine cranberry juice, water, honey, cinnamon, cloves and lemon peel in saucepan. Bring to a boil; simmer 15 minutes and strain. Add fruit juice, yeast flakes and lemon juice; heat gently. *(Do not boil!)* Serve in preheated mugs or cups, with a little nutmeg sprinkled over top of each serving. (Best of all in cold weather!) Serves 4-6.

HOLIDAY CAUDLE

6 egg yolks
4 cups fruit juice
6 cups strong herb tea
½ cup honey
1 teaspoon yeast flakes
Grated nutmeg

Beat egg yolks until light and lemon colored. Add fruit juice and herb tea; beat with rotary beater. Add honey and yeast flakes. Heat in double boiler. Serve in heated mugs, topped with a sprinkling of grated nutmeg. Serves 8-10.

Note: Caudles were popular in 17th-century England, when they were served in small two-handled silver cups as a warming refreshment. They are just as delicious today as a relaxing cold-weather drink.

HOLIDAY GLOG

1 *quart cranberry juice*
1 *quart orange juice*
1 *cup honey*
24 *whole cloves*
12 *cardamom seeds*
2 *or 3 sticks cinnamon*
1 *cup sun-dried raisins*
1 *cup blanched, unsalted almonds*
1 *tablespoon yeast flakes*

Combine all ingredients in saucepan. Heat to just below boiling. Serve in preheated mugs or glasses. Serves 20.

WINTER HOT PUNCH

12 *whole cloves*
1 *large orange, unpeeled*
1 *tablespoon honey*
1 *tablespoon yeast flakes*
1 *quart apple juice*
1 *cup berry juice*

Stick cloves into orange. Toast orange over an open fire until light brown. Cut orange into slices; place in saucepan. Add honey, yeast flakes; briefly warm. Now add apple juice and berry juice. Let heat for just an instant. Serve in preheated cups. Serves 8-10.

VEGETABLE COCKTAIL

4 cups carrot juice
1 cup celery juice
1 teaspoon yeast flakes
Pinch of vegetized sea salt

Blend together. Serve comfortably cool. Serves 4-6.

TOMATO CABBAGE JUICE COOLER

3 cups tomato juice
1 cup cabbage juice
1 teaspoon yeast flakes
Pinch of vegetized sea salt

Blend together. Serve comfortably cold. Serves 4-6.

CARROT CELERY COCKTAIL

3 cups carrot juice
1 cup celery juice
Sprig or two of parsley
1 teaspoon yeast flakes
Pinch of vegetized salt

Combine carrot and celery juice; now add yeast flakes and blend. Add vegetized salt. Serve comfortably cold. Serves 4-6.

THREE-WAY VEGETABLE TONIC

⅔ cup carrot juice
1 tablespoon beet juice
⅓ cup celery juice
1 teaspoon yeast flakes
Pinch of vegetized salt

Combine carrot, beet and celery juices. Now add yeast flakes. Stir. Add vegetized salt. Stir thoroughly or blend. Serve comfortably cold. Serves 1-2.

HOT VEGETABLE BROTH

> *1 cup chicken, beef or vegetable broth*
> *1 teaspoon vegetable broth powder*
> *1 teaspoon yeast flakes*
> *Sea salt to taste*

Combine all ingredients and steam until piping hot. Serve promptly. Serves 1.

MAGNIFIQUE MILK SHAKE

> *1 cup milk*
> *1 teaspoon skim milk powder*
> *1 teaspoon yeast flakes*
> *1 teaspoon honey (more to taste if desired)*

Add to the above any *one* of any of these flavorings:

> *6 to 8 dates, depitted*
> *¼ cup dark sun-dried raisins*
> *¼ cup pitted prunes*
> *¼ cup pitted bing cherries*
> *¼ cup strawberries*
> *¼ cup blueberries*

Combine just *one* of the flavorings above to the first four listed items (milk, milk powder, yeast flakes, honey), blend or stir until smooth. Serve promptly. Serves 1.

CARROT-COCONUT MILK SHAKE

½ cup carrot juice
1 cup coconut juice, canned
⅓ cup skim milk powder
⅓ cup fine coconut flakes
1 teaspoon clover honey
1 teaspoon yeast flakes

Combine all ingredients. Blend or shake until smooth. Serve promptly. Serves 1-2.

CHAPTER 4

YEAST BREADS, ROLLS, MUFFINS, BISCUITS, PANCAKES, WAFFLES

PUMPERNICKEL BREAD

9 *cups unsifted whole grain flour*
3 *cups unsifted rye flour*
2 *tablespoons sea salt*
1 *tablespoon yeast flakes*
1 *cup whole bran cereal*
¾ *cup unbleached yellow corn meal*
2 *packages active dry yeast*
3½ *cups water*
¼ *cup dark molasses*
1 *tablespoon margarine*
2 *cups mashed potatoes (at room temperature)*
2 *teaspoons caraway seed*

Combine whole grain and rye flours. In a very large bowl, thoroughly mix 2 cups flour mixture, sea salt, yeast flakes, bran cereal, corn meal and undissolved yeast. Put aside.

Now combine water, molasses and margarine in a saucepan. Heat over low heat until liquids are very warm (120°F.–130°F.). Margarine does not need to melt.

Then gradually add this heated mixture to the dry ingredients and beat 2 minutes at medium speed of electric mixer, scraping bowl occasionally. Add potatoes and 1 cup flour mixture. Beat at high speed 2 minutes, scraping bowl occasionally. Stir in caraway seed and enough flour mixture to make a soft dough. Turn out onto lightly floured board; cover and let rest 15 minutes. Then knead until smooth and elastic—about 15 minutes. Place in greased bowl, turning to grease top. Cover; let rise in warm place, free from draft, until doubled in bulk, about 1 hour. Punch dough down; let rise again 30 minutes. Punch dough down again; turn out onto lightly floured board. Divide into 3 equal pieces. Shape into round balls. Place in 3 oiled 8- or 9-inch round cake pans. Cover; let rise in warm place, free from draft, until doubled in bulk, about 45 minutes. Bake at 350°F. about 50 minutes, or until done. Remove from pans and cool on wire racks. Makes 3 loaves.

CRACKED WHEAT BREAD

4¾ to 5¾ cups unsifted whole grain flour
2 tablespoons honey
4 teaspoons salt substitute or vegetized salt
2 packages active dry yeast
1 tablespoon yeast flakes
1½ cups water
½ cup milk
3 tablespoons margarine
1 cup cracked wheat

In a large bowl, thoroughly mix 2 cups flour, honey, salt substitute, undissolved active dry yeast and yeast flakes.

Then combine water, milk and margarine in a saucepan. Heat over low heat until liquids are very warm (120°F.–130°F.). Margarine does not need to melt. Gradually add to dry ingredients and beat 2 minutes at medium speed of electric mixer, scraping bowl occasionally. Add cracked wheat and beat at high speed 2 minutes, scraping bowl occasionally. Stir in enough flour to make a soft dough. Turn out onto lightly floured board; knead until smooth and elastic, about 8 to 10 minutes. Place in oiled bowl, turning to oil top. Cover; let rise in warm place, free from draft, until doubled in bulk, about 1 hour.

Punch dough down. Turn out onto lightly floured board. Cover; let rest on board 15 minutes. Divide dough in half. Roll each half to a 12 x 8-inch rectangle. Shape into loaves. Place in 2 oiled 8½ x 4½ x 2½-inch loaf pans. Cover; let rise in warm place, free from draft, until doubled in bulk, about 1 hour. Then bake at 400°F. about 30 minutes, or until

done. Remove from pans and cool on wire racks.
Makes 2 loaves.

OLDE-FASHIONED RYE ROLLS

½ cup warm water (105°F.–115°F.)
2 packages active dry yeast
1½ cups warm milk (105°F.–115°F.)
1 tablespoon honey
1 tablespoon vegetized salt
1 tablespoon yeast flakes
¼ cup molasses
2 tablespoons margarine
3 to 3½ cups unsifted whole grain flour
2½ cups unsifted rye flour
Melted margarine
Peanut oil
1 egg white, beaten
2 teaspoons caraway seed
1 teaspoon sea salt

Measure warm water into large warm bowl. Sprinkle
in yeast; stir until dissolved. Add warm milk, honey,
vegetized salt, yeast flakes, molasses, and 2 tablespoons margarine. Add 2 cups whole grain flour.
Beat with rotary beater until smooth (about 1 min-
ute). Add 1 cup rye flour. Beat vigorously with a
wooden spoon until smooth (about 150 strokes).
Stir in remaining rye flour and additional whole
grain flour to make a soft dough. Turn out onto
lightly floured board and knead until smooth and
elastic, about 8 to 10 minutes. Cover with plastic
wrap, then a towel. Let rest 20 minutes.

Now divide dough into 4 equal portions. Roll each

portion into a 6 x 14-inch rectangle on a lightly floured board. Brush with melted margarine. Crease dough at 2-inch intervals with blunt edge of knife, beginning at 6-inch edge. Fold dough back and forth on crease lines, accordion fashion. Cut folded dough into 1-inch pieces. Place cut side down in oiled muffin cups. Brush rolls with peanut oil. Cover pans loosely with plastic wrap. Refrigerate 2 to 24 hours.

When ready to bake, remove from refrigerator. Uncover dough carefully. Let stand uncovered 10 minutes at room temperature. Brush rolls with beaten egg white and sprinkle with caraway seed and 1 teaspoon sea salt. Bake at 375°F. 20 to 25 minutes, or until done. Makes 24 rolls.

DELICIOUS DINNER ROLLS

10 to 12 cups unsifted whole grain flour
½ cup honey
4 teaspoons sea salt
1 tablespoon yeast flakes
2 packages active dry yeast
1½ cups milk
1½ cups water
½ cup (1 stick) margarine

In a large bowl, thoroughly mix 3 cups flour, honey, sea salt, yeast flakes and undissolved active dry yeast.

Combine milk, water and margarine in a saucepan. Heat over low heat until liquids are very warm (120°F.–130°F.). Margarine does not need to melt. Gradually add to dry ingredients and beat 2 minutes at medium speed of electric mixer, scraping bowl occasionally. Add 2 cups flour. Beat at high speed 2 minutes, scraping bowl occasionally. Stir in enough additional flour to make a soft dough. Turn out onto lightly floured board; knead until smooth and elastic, about 8 to 10 minutes. Place in oiled bowl, turning to oil top. Cover; let rise in warm place, free from draft, until doubled in bulk, about 1 hour.

Punch dough down; turn out onto lightly floured board. Divide dough into 4 equal pieces. Shape into rolls. Place on oiled baking sheets about 2 inches apart. Cover; let rise in warm place, free from draft, until almost doubled in bulk, about 45 minutes.

Bake at 275°F. 20 to 25 minutes, or until rolls just start to change color. Cool on sheets for 20 minutes. Remove from pans or sheets and finish cooling on wire racks. NOTE: Now you may wrap tightly in plastic bags and refrigerate overnight or up to 1 week for regular use. Just before serving, place rolls on ungreased baking sheet. Bake at 400°F. 10 to 12 minutes, or until golden brown. If desired, brush with melted margarine. Makes 48 rolls.

ENGLISH MUFFINS

1 cup milk
2 tablespoons honey
1 teaspoon sea salt
1 tablespoon yeast flakes
3 tablespoons margarine
1 cup warm water (105°F.–115°F.)
1 package active dry yeast
5 to 6 cups unsifted flour
Natural corn meal

Scald milk; stir in honey, sea salt, yeast flakes and margarine. Cool to lukewarm. Measure warm water into large warm bowl. Sprinkle in active dry yeast; stir until dissolved. Stir in lukewarm milk mixture and 3 cups flour; beat until smooth. Add enough additional flour to make a stiff dough. Turn out onto lightly floured board; knead about 2 minutes or until dough is manageable and can be formed into a ball. (Dough may be slightly sticky.) Place in oiled bowl, turning to oil top. Cover; let rise in warm place, free from draft, until doubled in bulk, about 1 hour.

Punch dough down; divide in half. On a board heavily sprinkled with corn meal, pat each half of the dough into ½-inch thickness. Cut into circles with a floured 3-inch cookie cutter. Place on ungreased baking sheets about 2 inches apart. Cover; let rise in warm place, free from draft, until doubled in bulk, about ½ hour.

Place on a lightly oiled medium-hot griddle or skillet, corn meal side down. Bake until well browned, about 10 minutes on each side. Cool on wire racks. To serve, split muffins in half and toast. Makes about 18 muffins.

WHOLE BRAN MUFFINS

¾ cup whole bran cereal
⅓ cup honey
1½ teaspoons vegetized salt
½ cup (1 stick) margarine
1 tablespoon yeast flakes
½ cup boiling water
½ cup warm water (105°F.–115°F.)
2 packages active dry yeast
1 egg, beaten
3¾ cups unsifted whole grain flour
Melted margarine

Combine cereal, honey, salt, margarine and yeast flakes in a bowl. Add boiling water; stir until margarine is melted. Set aside to cool until lukewarm.

Measure warm water into large prewarmed bowl. Sprinkle in active dry yeast; stir until dissolved. Add lukewarm cereal mixture, egg and enough flour to make a stiff dough. Turn out onto lightly floured board; knead until smooth and elastic, about 8 to 10 minutes. Place in oiled bowl, turning to oil top. Cover; let rise in warm place, free from draft, until doubled in bulk, about 1 hour.

Punch dough down; divide in half. Divide each half into 12 equal pieces. Form each piece into a smooth round ball. Place in oiled muffin pans, 2½ x 1½ inches, or in 2 oiled 8-inch round cake pans. Brush muffins with melted margarine. Cover; let rise in warm place, free from draft, until doubled in bulk, about 1 hour. Now bake at 375°F. 20 to 25 minutes, or until done. Remove from pans and cool on wire racks. Serve warm. Makes 24 muffins.

BEATEN CREAM BISCUITS

1 cup whole wheat flour
2 cups whole wheat pastry flour
2 tablespoons yeast flakes
1 teaspoon vegetized salt
¾ cup heavy cream
¾ cup vegetable oil

Sift both flours and yeast flakes and salt into a mixing bowl. Now stir milk and oil into flour slowly. When thoroughly mixed, place dough on bread board. Roll out and fold dough over and over, rolling each time. Beat in between times, rolling, folding and beating. Then roll out to ¾-inch or biscuit thickness. Cut with biscuit cutter; stick with fork. Lay on oiled cookie sheet. Bake at 350°F. for about 15 to 20 minutes. Makes about 12 biscuits.

BUTTERFLAKE BISCUITS

2 yeast cakes
1½ cups lukewarm milk
⅓ cup vegetable oil
1 teaspoon salt substitute
¼ cup honey
1 teaspoon yeast flakes
2 cups unbleached pastry flour
2½ cups unbleached flour

Crumble yeast cakes into milk. Add honey and yeast flakes and set aside for a few minutes. Now add oil, salt substitute and gradually sift in the flour. Beat vigorously. Cover. Set aside to rise to double its bulk. Roll to 1/4-inch biscuit thickness, cut in 2-inch strips. Brush with oil or melted margarine. Pile 5 or 6 strips together. Cut in squares. Place in oiled biscuit tins. Cover, let rise until light. Bake at 425°F. for 15 to 20 minutes. Makes about 12 biscuits.

PANCAKE BLINI

Pancakes:
1 egg
3/4 cup milk
1 cup pancake mix
1 tablespoon yeast flakes
1 tablespoon butter or margarine

Topping:
1 cup sour cream
1 tablespoon minced raw onion
Chopped hard-cooked egg

Beat egg until foamy, add with milk to pancake mix and stir in yeast flakes. Keep stirring until well blended. Let stand 30 minutes. Melt a little of the butter in a hot skillet heated to 400°F. Make pancakes 1 1/2 to 2 inches in diameter, adding more butter to skillet if needed before each batch. Serve warm topped with a spoonful of dairy sour cream blended with minced onion and chopped egg. (Pancake blinis may be kept warm—wrapped in foil—in oven until time to serve.) Makes about 20 pancake blinis.

CINNAMON-APPLE PANCAKES

    1 large tart apple
    1 tablespoon honey
    1 tablespoon lemon juice
    1 cup packaged pancake mix
    1 tablespoon yeast flakes
    1 cup milk
    1 egg
    1 tablespoon oil or melted shortening
    2 tablespoons butter or margarine
    Cinnamon
    Yogurt or whipped cream

Peel and core apple, slice very thin; cover with honey and lemon juice. Let stand while preparing batter. Combine pancake mix, yeast flakes, milk, egg, oil; beat lightly until fairly smooth.

Melt 1 tablespoon of the butter in ovenproof 10-inch skillet, rotating skillet so butter covers sides. Pour in the pancake batter, cook over low heat until it begins to bubble. Reduce heat, top with apple slices. Continue to cook over low heat until edges of pancake begin to firm. Sprinkle top of pancake with cinnamon. Dot with remaining 1 tablespoon butter. Place under preheated broiler, 4 to 6 inches from heat, about 5 minutes, until top of pancake is glazed. Cut in wedges. Serve warm as dessert, topped with yogurt or whipped cream. Serves 4 to 6.

PECAN WAFFLES

1 cup milk
1 egg
2 tablespoons oil or melted shortening
¼ cup chopped pecans
1 tablespoon yeast flakes
1 cup packaged buttermilk
    pancake mix

Combine milk, egg, oil, pecans, yeast flakes and pancake mix. (If melted shortening is used, add after pancake mix.) Beat until batter is well-blended. Pour batter into hot waffle iron, and bake until steaming stops. Serve hot with butter and natural maple syrup. Makes 3 large waffles.

CHEESE WAFFLES

1¾ cups packaged buttermilk pancake mix
½ cup cold water
1 cup milk
⅔ cup grated sharp cheese
1 tablespoon yeast flakes
1 teaspoon salt substitute

Combine pancake mix, water and milk, beat well with rotary beater until fairly smooth; add grated cheese, yeast flakes and salt substitute. Bake in preheated waffle iron until crisp. Makes 6 waffles.

CHAPTER 5

MEAT DISHES

MIGHTY MEAT LOAF

1½ pounds chopped beef
½ cup buckwheat groats
2 eggs, unbeaten
1 medium onion, chopped
½ green pepper, chopped
1½ teaspoons salt substitute
1 teaspoon yeast flakes
1 cup tomato wedges

Combine all ingredients; mix lightly. Pack into oiled
9 x 5 x 3-inch loaf pan. Bake in moderate oven
(325°F.) 1½ hours. Serves 4 to 6.

VEAL AND PEPPERS

1 lb. boneless veal (rump, shoulder or leg, cut into 1½-inch pieces)

3 green and 1 medium-size peppers, seeded and cut into 1-inch strips

4 tablespoons oil

1 tablespoon yeast flakes

¼ lb. mushrooms, sliced

1 cup tomato wedges (or tomato puree)

Preheat oven to 325°F. Steam peppers in 2 table-spoons oil for about 10 minutes. The darkish spots that develop help contribute to the good flavor of the dish. Remove peppers from pan. In the same pan, brown veal cubes in the remaining oil. Add yeast flakes, mushrooms, cook for about 10 minutes. Add tomatoes and peppers. Cover and bake about 1 hour. Serves 3 to 4.

SIMPLE LAMB STEW

3 to 4 lbs. lamb shoulder or breast, cut in
   1-inch cubes
2 teaspoons salt substitute
1 tablespoon yeast flakes
1½ teaspoons unbleached flour
2 tablespoons shortening or cooking oil
2 whole cloves
¼ teaspoon thyme
1 clove garlic, minced
1 bay leaf
½ cup water
½ cup lemon juice
6 small onions, peeled
12 small potatoes
1 cup green beans

Season meat with salt substitute; dust with flour.
Now place all remaining ingredients except vegetables with meat in Dutch oven or deep skillet. Cover
tightly. Bring to a boil. Reduce heat and simmer
over slow fire for 1 hour. Add onions, potatoes and
beans; cook until tender, about 30 minutes longer.
Serves 6.

BALKAN LAMB IN A DISH

4 to 5 lb. lamb shoulder roast
1 clove garlic, pressed
8 medium carrots, pared
4 medium potatoes, pared
1 large eggplant, quartered
8 small pearl onions
2 tablespoons yeast flakes
4 zucchini, halved
¼ cup finely chopped celery tops
1 (1 lb. 13 oz.) can solid pack tomatoes (drained)
Parsley sprig
1 bay leaf

Place prepared vegetables in two-quart casserole; sprinkle with chopped celery tops. Place lamb, skin side up, on top of vegetables; add yeast flakes, tomatoes, parsley and bay leaf. Cover tightly. Cook in oven at 350°F. about 1½ hours or until lamb is fork-tender. Remove lid and brown another 30 minutes. Serve with brown rice. Serves 4 to 6.

LIVER AND ONIONS

4 large onions
½ teaspoon salt substitute
1 tablespoon oil
1 lb. calves' or baby beef liver
1 tablespoon yeast flakes
2 tablespoons orange juice

Cut onions into small pieces, add salt substitute and steam in oil until golden. Cut liver into 1-inch cubes, discarding skin and veins. Add liver and yeast flakes to onions, cooking and stirring a few minutes longer. Orange juice may be added just before serving. Serves 4.

FLAVORFUL BEEF ROAST

  5 *lbs. beef roast*
  2 *cups fruit juice*
  1 *clove garlic, minced*
  1 *large onion, quartered*
  1 *tablespoon oregano*
  1 *tablespoon yeast flakes*
  ½ *cup lemon juice*

Stick roast deeply with an ice pick on all sides, reaching to the center. Now mix marinade in a glass bowl, preferably a narrow, deep one capable of holding the roast. Combine all remaining ingredients and mix well. Place roast in marinade. Cover and refrigerate eight to ten hours. Turn meat several times. When ready to cook, place roast and marinade in covered baking dish. Bake in moderate oven (350°F.) about 2½ hours. Serves 8 to 10.

WESTERN STYLE HASH

1/3 cup butter
2 1/2 cups roast beef, cut in 1/4-inch cubes
2 cups raw potatoes, cut in 1/4-inch cubes
1 medium onion, chopped
1/2 cup thick beef gravy (or one-half 10 1/2-
    oz. can of beef with barley soup)
1/8 teaspoon thyme
2 tablespoons yeast flakes
Dash garlic powder
1/2 cup fruit juice
1/2 teaspoon salt substitute

Melt butter in heavy skillet. Mix all remaining ingredients; turn into skillet. Place skillet in a moderate oven (350°F.); bake 1 1/2 hours, turning 3 to 4 times with spatula. Serve with fresh raw salad. Serves 4 to 6.

CHAPTER 6

FISH

TUNA-YOGURT CASSEROLE

2 *cups canned tuna, drained*
1 *tablespoon lemon juice*
Dash paprika
½ *teaspoon yeast flakes*
1 *cup yogurt*
1 *tablespoon whole grain flour*
Thin lemon slices
Parsley

Break tuna in large chunks. Sprinkle with lemon juice, paprika and yeast flakes. Mix together with yogurt. Pour into oiled 1-quart casserole and bake in slow oven, 325°F., 40 minutes. Serve garnished with lemon slices and parsley. Serves 6.

BAKED FISH

(Use striped bass, red snapper, carp, mackerel
or other fish)

 2 *lbs. fish*
 2 *medium-sized onions*
 1 *No. 2 can tomatoes*
 1 *clove garlic, crushed*
 6 *tablespoons oil*
 ½ *teaspoon paprika*
 1 *tablespoon yeast flakes*
 Juice of ½ lemon
 Salt substitute
 Chopped parsley
 Lemon slices

Cut onions into slices and brown in 4 tablespoons of oil until golden brown. Add tomatoes, garlic, paprika, yeast flakes, lemon juice and remaining oil, salt substitute. Cook about 20 minutes. Place fish in baking dish and cover with this sauce. Bake in preheated oven at 400°F. about 30 minutes. Before serving, garnish with chopped parsley and lemon slices. Serves 4.

PAN FRIED FISH

(Use fillets of fish, small fish steak or
small whole fish)

 1½ *lbs. fish*
 4 *tablespoons oil*
 1 *tablespoon lemon juice*
 1 *tablespoon yeast flakes*
 Salt substitute
 Whole grain flour

Season fish with salt substitute. Sprinkle with lemon juice. Dip the fish lightly in flour and cover with yeast flakes. Now heat oil in skillet. Cook fish until golden brown on both sides about 10 minutes. Serve with tomato juice. Serves 4.

POACHED FISH

(Use cod, halibut, salmon, whitefish, pike)
1½ lbs. fish
1½ teaspoons salt substitute
1 tablespoon yeast flakes
2 cups water
4 peppercorns
1 bay leaf
1 tablespoon lemon juice
1 tablespoon vinegar
1 medium onion

Cut fish into serving pieces. Rub salt substitute lightly on fish. Coat with yeast flakes. Place fish in saucepan. Add water, onion and seasonings. Bring to a boil. Cover and cook fish gently for about 20 minutes or until fish flakes when tested with a fork (do not boil). Serve with raw vegetable salad. Serves 4.

SALMON STEAK BAKED IN FRUIT JUICE

1 lb. fresh salmon slices 1½ inches thick
Salt substitute
1 tablespoon yeast flakes
1 cup fresh fruit juice
1 clove garlic, peeled and sliced (optional)
2 tablespoons oil
Juice of ½ lemon

Preheat oven to 400°F. Place salmon slices in baking pan, sprinkle with salt substitute. Coat with yeast flakes. Combine all remaining ingredients and pour over fish. Bake about 15 to 20 minutes or until fish flakes easily when tested with a fork. This fish is good either hot or cold. Serves 3.

BAKED TROUT

3 to 5 lbs. fresh whole trout
1 tablespoon yeast flakes
1 cup tomato wedges
2 tablespoons olive oil
2 tablespoons chopped parsley
1 small clove garlic, minced
½ cup fruit juice

Clean trout well; coat with yeast flakes. Place in baking dish. Cover with tomato wedges, olive oil, parsley and garlic. Bake in a hot oven (400°F.) for 30 to 40 minutes, or until fish flakes easily. Baste during baking with fruit juice. Serves 3 to 5.

BAKED FISH SALAD

⅔ cup salad dressing or natural
    mayonnaise
½ cup fruit juice
1 cup wheat germ
2 tablespoons yeast flakes
2 cups flaked, cooked or canned fish (hali-
    but, salmon or tuna)
2 hard-cooked eggs, coarsely chopped
½ cup chopped celery
2 tablespoons capers
2 tablespoons chopped parsley
1 tablespoon minced onion
Salt substitute to taste

Stir salad dressing and fruit juice together until
blended. Add ¾ cup of the wheat germ and yeast
flakes and all remaining ingredients into the salad
dressing-fruit juice mixture. Turn mixture into oiled
baking shells or individual casseroles. Sprinkle remaining wheat germ over the top. Bake in a moderate oven (350°F.) for 30 minutes. Serves 4.

BAKED SOLE PAPRIKA

1½ lbs. fillets of sole or other white fish
1 small onion, thinly sliced
2 tablespoons yeast flakes
1 cup dairy sour cream
1 tablespoon whole grain flour
⅓ cup fruit juice
½ teaspoon paprika
Salt substitute

51

Arrange fish in oiled shallow baking dish. Cover with onion slices. Mix in all other ingredients and pour over fish. Bake in moderately hot oven (375°F.) about 25 minutes, or until fish is tender. Serves 4.

CHAPTER 7

POULTRY

THREE-HERB CHICKEN WITH YEAST FLAKES

3 whole broiler-fryer chicken breasts
Salt substitute to taste
1 tablespoon yeast flakes
¼ teaspoon each: basil, tarragon and
*   thyme, divided*
Juice of ½ lemon or lime, divided
1 tablespoon vegetable oil

Halve chicken breasts. Place skin side down on aluminum foil-lined broiler pan. Sprinkle with salt substitute, half the herbs, half of the yeast flakes. Brush with part of the lemon juice; dot with half of the vegetable oil. Broil in moderate oven, 350°F., about 3 to 4 inches from heat, for 30 minutes. Turn over chicken breasts, add all remaining ingredients. Broil another 20 to 30 minutes. Serves 6.

LEMON-KISSED CHICKEN

1 frying chicken, cut in quarters
¼ cup lemon juice
¼ cup oil
½ teaspoon salt substitute
1 tablespoon yeast flakes
¼ teaspoon powdered thyme
⅛ teaspoon paprika
½ cup whole grain flour
¼ cup vegetable oil

Combine lemon juice, oil, yeast flakes and all seasonings to make a marinade. Pour over chicken. Be sure all chicken parts are in contact with marinade. Marinate for 1 hour in refrigerator. Drain chicken, dust with flour; heat oil in heavy skillet. Place chicken in hot oil and fry until golden brown on all sides. Place in moderate oven at 350°F. and bake about 30 minutes or until tender. Serves 4.

CHICKEN PAPRIKA

1 frying chicken, disjointed
4 tablespoons oil
2 medium-sized onions, sliced
2 teaspoons paprika
2 teaspoons yeast flakes
1 tablespoon whole wheat flour
¼ cup chicken broth or water
1 teaspoon lemon juice
Salt substitute

Preheat oven to 300°F. In deep skillet, brown onions in oil until golden; add paprika and yeast flakes and mix. Add chicken pieces, turning them until well coated with the onions. Sprinkle with desired salt substitute. Cover and bake at 300°F. for about 45 to 60 minutes. Remove chicken pieces. Keep warm. Mix flour with water and add to pan juices. Boil for a few minutes. Pour over chicken. Serve with natural brown rice. Serves 4.

CRISP CHICKEN

   1 *cup wheat germ*
   1 *teaspoon salt substitute*
   1 *teaspoon yeast flakes*
   1 *broiler-fryer chicken, cut in serving pieces*
  ½ *cup evaporated milk*

Combine wheat germ with salt substitute and yeast flakes. Line shallow baking pan with aluminum foil. Dip chicken pieces in evaporated milk, then roll immediately in dry mixture. Place chicken pieces, skin side up, in foil-lined pan; do not crowd. Bake in a moderate oven (350°F.) about 1 hour or until tender. No need to cover or turn chicken while cooking. Serves 4.

TSE BOU AKI
(Foil-Wrapped Chicken)

3 tablespoons soy sauce
3 tablespoons vegetable oil
1 tablespoon lemon juice
1 tablespoon sesame seeds
1 teaspoon honey
1 tablespoon yeast flakes
1 whole broiler-fryer chicken breast
2 broiler-fryer chicken legs
Parsley

Combine soy sauce, vegetable oil, lemon juice, sesame seeds, honey and yeast flakes. Now bone and skin chicken. Cut breast into 16 portions and legs into 8 portions each. Place chicken pieces in marinade 3 to 5 minutes. Place each portion in center of 6-inch square of heavy-duty aluminum foil. Add a sprig of parsley; bring the four ends together and twist to seal. Fry in hot deep oil (400°F.) 5 minutes only. Serve promptly. Makes about 30 appetizer servings.

BASIC SIMMERED CHICKEN

1 broiler-fryer chicken, whole or cut in serving pieces
2 cups water
1 small onion, sliced
2 celery tops
2 bay leaves
1 teaspoon yeast flakes
1 teaspoon salt substitute

Put chicken in kettle, add water and all remaining ingredients. Bring to a boil; cover tightly. Reduce heat and simmer 40 minutes. Remove from heat; strain broth. Now refrigerate chicken and broth at once. When chicken is cool, remove chicken from bones. Dice and place in cups. Makes about 3 cups diced cooked chicken and about 2 cups broth.

BRAISED CHICKEN ORIENTALA

1 frying chicken, cut in serving pieces
½ lb. mushroom caps
1 clove garlic, mashed
3 tablespoons vegetable oil
2 tablespoons fruit juice
2 tablespoons soy sauce
2 tablespoons yeast flakes

Brown chicken and garlic lightly in oil. Add mushrooms, cover and cook about five minutes. Add fruit juice, cook until entirely absorbed. Add soy sauce and yeast flakes. Cover and cook gently until chicken is tender, about 20 to 30 minutes. Serves 4.

MILANESE CHICKEN

1 whole chicken breast
1 egg white
Ginger
1 tablespoon paprika
1 tablespoon whole grain flour
3 tablespoons wheat germ
1 tablespoon yeast flakes
Vegetable oil
1 tablespoon grated Parmesan cheese

Bone and take the skin off the chicken breast. Pound or flatten slightly. Dust with flour. Lightly mix ginger and paprika with egg white. Dip meat into egg white. Coat with wheat germ and yeast flakes mixed with cheese. Let stand 5 to 10 minutes. Brown in oil until crisp, about 5 minutes on each side. Serves 2.

CHAPTER 8

EGGS

COTTAGE CHEESE SCRAMBLED EGGS

1 tablespoon butter
1 teaspoon salt substitute
½ teaspoon yeast flakes
½ cup milk
6 eggs
½ cup cottage cheese

Melt butter in medium skillet over low heat. Add salt substitute, yeast flakes and milk to eggs; beat lightly. Pour into skillet. Cook over low heat, stirring until eggs are creamy and firm, but not dry. Gently fold in cheese. Continue cooking over very low heat, only until cheese is warm but not hot. Serve promptly. Serves 4.

EGGFUL HALF-MOONS

6 eggs
½ teaspoon salt substitute
¼ teaspoon paprika
1 tablespoon yeast flakes
¼ cup grated sharp cheese
¼ cup grated carrots
¼ cup finely chopped pimiento
¼ cup finely chopped green pepper
¼ cup wheat germ

Beat eggs, salt substitute, paprika and yeast flakes
until thick and lemon colored. Heat a lightly greased
griddle until a drop of water sizzles on the griddle.
Pour eggs onto the griddle in four equal amounts.
Sprinkle with 1 tablespoon of your desired seasonings such as cheese, carrots, pimiento, green pepper,
wheat germ or use all of them. When omelet is set,
fold in half to form a half-moon shape. Serve promptly. Serves 4.

QUICK EGG SOUFFLÉ

1½ cups milk
2 tablespoons butter
6 eggs
1 teaspoon salt substitute
1 tablespoon yeast flakes
Parsley

Heat milk and butter in upper part of double boiler.
Add seasoning and yeast flakes to eggs and beat until very light. Add eggs to the hot milk and blend

60

well. Cook over gently simmering water for 30 minutes. Serve on warm plates. Garnish with a sprig of parsley or snipped parsley. Serves 6.

FLUFFY EGG NESTS

    4 *slices hot, buttered toast*
    4 *egg whites*
    4 *egg yolks*
    ½ *to 1 cup grated, sharp cheese*
    1 *tablespoon yeast flakes*
    Salt substitute

Beat egg whites until stiff, but not dry. Place hot, buttered toast on cookie sheet. Pile whites on toast, making an indentation in the center of each. Carefully slip an egg yolk into each indentation. Sprinkle with cheese, yeast flakes, salt substitute. Bake in a 350°F. (moderate) oven for 15 minutes or until whites are lightly browned and yolks are set. Serves 4.

PARMESAN EGGS

    2 *tablespoons butter*
    2 *tablespoons berry juice*
    2 *eggs*
    1 *teaspoon yeast flakes*
    Salt substitute
    2 *tablespoons parmesan cheese*

Brown butter in skillet; add berry juice. Bring to a boil. Now break eggs into mixture. Season with yeast flakes and salt substitute. When egg whites begin to set, remove skillet from heat. Sprinkle with cheese.

Place skillet under broiler and brown cheese. (Cheese browns quickly, so watch closely.) Serves 2.

EGGS WITH CHEESE

½ cup cream
2 tablespoons oil
1 (3 oz.) package cream cheese, softened
6 eggs
1 teaspoon salt substitute
1 teaspoon yeast flakes
3 tablespoons orange juice

Heat cream over low heat in a skillet or chafing dish along with oil and cream cheese. Stir with a fork until a smooth, creamy consistency is reached. Beat eggs just until blended; add to cream mixture. Season with salt. Add yeast flakes. Cook and stir over low heat until egg mixture is softly scrambled. Just before serving, stir in orange juice. Makes an ideal breakfast dish. Serves 3 to 4.

EGGSTRA GOOD

3 egg yolks
1 cup cream
Salt substitute
1 tablespoon yeast flakes
4 hard-cooked eggs, quartered
½ cup fruit juice

Beat yolks in cream; season with salt substitute. Add yeast flakes. Cook over hot water in top of double boiler until thick. Add quartered eggs. When ready to serve, stir in fruit juice. Serve in hot ramekins. Serves 2 to 4.

CHAPTER 9

DAIRY

NO-COOK CHEESE MAGNIFIQUE

3 cups (12 ounces) shredded Cheddar cheese
⅓ cup crumbled Blue cheese
½ cup plain yogurt
1 teaspoon yeast flakes
¼ cup minced ripe olives
½ cup chopped nuts
¼ cup chopped parsley

In a small mixing bowl, beat together Cheddar and Blue cheese until smooth. Add yeast flakes and yogurt and beat until creamy. Stir in olives. Cover and chill. Shape into ball. Roll in nuts and parsley. Return to refrigerator. Allow to come to room temperature before serving. Slice into desired portions. Serves 4 to 6.

CORN AND CHEESE FONDUE

½ cup wheat germ or bread crumbs
4 tablespoons yeast flakes
1½ cups cream-style corn
2 teaspoons chopped green pepper
½ cup hot milk
¾ cup finely grated cheese of your choice
½ teaspoon salt substitute
2 eggs, well-beaten

Combine all ingredients. Pour mixture into oiled loaf pan and set briefly in pan of hot water. Remove. Bake at 350°F. until set, or about 1 hour. Serves 2 to 4.

COTTAGE CHEESE LOAF

2 cups cottage cheese
2 cups soft bread crumbs
2 cups chopped nut meats
4 tablespoons yeast flakes
1½ teaspoons salt substitute
½ teaspoon onion juice
Juice of 1 lemon
2 tablespoons butter or margarine

Combine all ingredients. Place in well-oiled baking pan and bake in moderately hot oven (370°F.) about 30 minutes. Serve promptly. Serves 4-6.

PEANUT CHEESE LOAF

⅔ cup cooked oatmeal, wheat cereal or
   brown rice
¼ cup chopped green pepper
3 tablespoons minced onion
1 teaspoon salt substitute
4 tablespoons yeast flakes
1 egg, well beaten
2 teaspoons lemon juice
1 cup chopped unsalted peanuts
⅔ cup fine bread crumbs or wheat germ
1 cup grated American cheese
⅓ cup milk

Combine all ingredients. Place mixture in oiled loaf
pan and bake in moderate oven (350°F.) about 1
hour. Serve very hot. Serves 4 to 6.

SCALLOPED RICE AND CHEESE

2 tablespoons butter or margarine
6 medium-sized onions, chopped
1½ cups uncooked brown rice
1½ teaspoons salt substitute
1 tablespoon yeast flakes
2½ cups boiling water
2 cups condensed tomato soup
1 chopped green pepper
1 cup American cheese, diced

Melt butter in skillet and steam onions in it until golden brown. Add rice, salt substitute and yeast flakes. Cook until rice is nearly tender. Add tomato soup. When rice has absorbed all the liquid gently, stir in green pepper and cheese. Pour into well-oiled baking dish. Bake in moderate oven (350°F.) about 15 minutes. Serves 4 to 6.

CHEESE-PUMPKIN PIE

1 cup cottage cheese
¾ cup honey
1 teaspoon ground ginger
1 teaspoon ground cinnamon
⅛ teaspoon ground cloves
1 teaspoon yeast flakes
½ teaspoon salt substitute
2 cups canned pumpkin
3 eggs, well beaten
1½ cups milk, scalded
10-inch unbaked pastry shell

Beat cottage cheese with rotary beater until almost smooth. Next combine honey, spices, yeast flakes, salt substitute. Add to pumpkin, eggs and cottage cheese. Mix until blended. Stir in scalded milk. Pour into pastry shell. Bake in moderate oven (350°F.) from 50 to 60 minutes, or until set. Serves 10.

CHEESE-'N'-YEAST CASSEROLE

1 egg, beaten
1 cup brown buckwheat groats
2 tablespoons yeast flakes
1 teaspoon salt substitute
1 large onion, chopped
¼ cup vegetable oil
2 cups water
1 cup cottage cheese
½ cup shredded Cheddar cheese
Paprika

Combine egg, groats, yeast flakes, salt substitute. Next, in medium-size skillet, brown onion in oil for 3 minutes. Now stir in groat mixture and water; bring to a boil. Cook, tightly covered, over low heat 15 minutes. Add cottage cheese; toss lightly to mix well. Turn into 1½ quart baking dish; sprinkle with Cheddar cheese and paprika. Place in broiler under low heat for 5 minutes or until Cheddar cheese is melted. Serves 4 to 6.

CHAPTER 10

FRUIT SALADS

FRUIT BLOSSOM SALAD

3 red apples
2 grapefruits
4 large oranges
½ pound grapes
Watercress
½ teaspoon yeast flakes
Apple cider vinegar dressing

Core apples; do not pare. Slice. Section grapefruit and oranges. Halve and seed grapes. Arrange alternate slices of fruits petal-wise on salad plates. Heap center with grapes. Garnish with watercress. Mix yeast flakes with dressing and sprinkle over salad. Serves 6.

AMBROSIA SALAD

1 cup orange sections
½ cup seedless grape halves
¼ cup chopped dates
1 cup cottage cheese
¼ cup yogurt
1 banana, sliced
1 tablespoon yeast flakes
Lettuce
¼ cup shredded coconut

Combine orange sections, grapes and dates and chill. Now press cheese through a fine sieve. Add yogurt, banana and mix together with yeast flakes. Fold chilled fruits into cheese mixture. Serve on crisp lettuce. Sprinkle each serving with coconut. Serves 4.

BANANA SPLIT SALAD

Banana
Lettuce
Yogurt
Crushed strawberries
Chopped nuts
1 tablespoon yeast flakes
Whole strawberries

Peel banana and split lengthwise. Arrange, cut side up, on lettuce. Top with 2 generous spoonfuls (or scoops) of yogurt. Spoon crushed strawberries over each mound. Sprinkle with chopped nuts, yeast flakes. Garnish with whole strawberries. Serves 1.

FIG, ORANGE AND CHEESE SALAD

½ cup sun-dried figs or dates, cut small
2 cups diced oranges, well drained
1 cup cottage cheese
1 teaspoon yeast flakes
Lettuce or other greens

Combine figs, oranges and cottage cheese. Mix very lightly. Sprinkle with yeast flakes. Serve on lettuce or other greens. If desired, sprinkle with chopped nuts. Serves 6.

FLORIDA FRUIT SALAD

4 oranges, sectioned
1 large grapefruit, sectioned
1 avocado
Romaine or other greens
1 teaspooon yeast flakes
2 cups cottage cheese
Whole cooked cranberries
Yogurt

Arrange sections of orange and grapefruit and slices of avocado on romaine or other greens in fan shape. Sprinkle with yeast flakes. Top with spoonfuls of cottage cheese. Garnish with whole cooked cranberries. Serve with yogurt. Serves 6.

GRAPEFRUIT SALAD BOWL

2 grapefruits
Salad greens
Cottage cheese
½ cup small apricot slices
Watercress
1 tablespoon yeast flakes
¼ cup very thin strips of Cheddar cheese

Cut grapefruits in half. Remove sections; cut in bite-size pieces; chill. Scrape out grapefruit shells with spoon. Line shells with pieces of salad greens. Spoon tall mound of cottage cheese in center of each shell. Sprinkle with yeast flakes. Surround with mounds of grapefruit, apricot, watercress, cheese strips. Serves 4.

PEACH MELBA SALAD

1 peach half
1 lettuce cup
⅓ cup cottage cheese
1 tablespoon raspberry preserves
½ teaspoon yeast flakes
1 tablespoon yogurt
1 sprig watercress

Put peach half, cut-side up, in lettuce cup. Fill pit cavity with cottage cheese. Top with preserves, yeast flakes and yogurt. Garnish with a sprig of watercress. Serves 1.

CHAPTER 11

VEGETABLE SALADS

ZESTY POTATO SALAD

5 cups sliced cooked potatoes
½ cup chopped celery
¼ cup thinly sliced radishes
¼ cup finely chopped onion
¼ cup low-calorie French dressing
1 teaspoon yeast flakes
1½ cups yogurt

Mix together potatoes, celery, radishes and onions. Sprinkle in yeast flakes. Stir in French dressing and chill 2 to 3 hours. Just before serving, gradually stir in yogurt. TIP: If desired, garnish with chopped chives. Serves 8 to 10.

TOSSED SPINACH SALAD

1 cup coarsely shredded raw spinach
1 cup bite-size pieces raw cauliflower
⅓ cup grated raw carrot
½ cup yogurt
Salt substitute
½ teaspoon yeast flakes

Toss spinach, cauliflower and carrot. Fold in yogurt. Season with salt substitute and yeast flakes. Serves 4.

TUNA SPRING SALAD

2 tablespoons chopped olives
½ cup shredded carrot
½ cup chopped celery
¼ cup chopped parsley
1 small onion, finely chopped
1 tablespoon apple cider vinegar
1 cup cottage cheese
1 tablespoon yeast flakes
1¼ cups drained canned tuna
Salt substitute
Lettuce

Mix olives, carrot, celery, parsley, onion and vinegar. Now mix cottage cheese and yeast flakes. Next break tuna into large flakes with fork. Add vegetable and cheese mixtures. Toss lightly. Season with salt substitute. Serve on lettuce. Serves 4.

LIME CUCUMBER SALAD

3 oz. package (6 tablespoons) lime-flavored
    gelatin
1 cup hot water
¼ cup apple cider vinegar
1 teaspoon salt substitute
1 tablespoon yeast flakes
1 teaspoon grated onion
1 cup sour cream
1 medium cucumber, coarsely grated
Lettuce

Dissolve gelatin in hot water. Add vinegar, salt substitute, yeast flakes and onion. Chill until gelatin
begins to thicken. Stir in some sour cream and cucumber. Then add the balance. Pour into 6 individual molds. Chill until firm. Unmold on lettuce.
Serves 6.

TURKEY SALAD

2 cups diced cooked turkey
1½ cups diced cooked chicken
½ cup yogurt
3 tablespoons salad oil
1 tablespoon yeast flakes
Salt substitute
1 tablespoon capers

Combine all ingredients. Thoroughly mix together.
Serve chilled on raw salad greens. Serves 6.

EGG AND WATERCRESS SALAD

1 hard-cooked egg for each serving
Stuffed olives, thinly sliced
1 teaspoon yeast flakes
Watercress

Place fresh, chilled watercress on individual salad plates. Sprinkle with yeast flakes. Top with sliced egg, then with sliced olives. Serve with desired salad dressing. Serves 1.

HOT COLESLAW

3 cups shredded cabbage
1 tablespoon butter or margarine
1 egg, well beaten
¼ cup cider vinegar plus water to make ⅔ cup liquid
½ cup cream, sweet or sour
1 tablespoon yeast flakes

Heat butter, beaten egg and vinegar-water solution in double boiler. Add cream and yeast flakes and stir until mixture coats spoon. Pour this hot sauce over cabbage just before serving. Serves 4 to 6.

CHAPTER 12

SOUPS

LIMA BEAN SOUP

1 *cup cooked lima beans*
3 *carrots*
½ *cup uncooked natural brown rice*
3 *small onions*
1 *teaspoon yeast flakes*
1 *tablespoon butter or margarine*

Cut carrots and onions into small pieces. Add rice and yeast flakes and cook in small amount of water until tender. Put lima beans through sieve. Add to mixture. Add butter. (*Note:* If soup is too thick, add a little more freshly boiled water.) TIP: Leftover lima beans or navy beans may be used with this recipe. Serves 4.

BARLEY SOUP

¾ cup pearl barley
6 cups water
½ cup diced carrots
½ cup diced onions
½ cup diced celery
½ cup cooked peas
¾ cup fresh or canned tomatoes
⅛ lb. butter or margarine
1 tablespoon yeast flakes
Salt substitute to taste

Cook barley in 3 cups water until tender. Drain and save barley water. Boil celery and onions together in remaining 3 cups water for 30 minutes. Add carrots and boil for another 30 minutes. Add peas and tomatoes. Simmer for 25 minutes. Add cooked barley, barley water, butter, yeast flakes. Season with salt substitute. Serves 8.

CHEESE SOUP

1 tablespoon chopped onion
1 tablespoon butter or margarine
1 tablespoon flour
3 cups milk
1 teaspoon yeast flakes
¾ cup grated American cheddar cheese

Melt butter. Add onion and cook slowly until onion is yellow. Stir in flour, add milk and yeast flakes and bring to boiling point. Strain, add cheese and stir until cheese melts. Serve sprinkled with paprika and tiny sprig of parsley on each bowl. Serves 4.

DRIED GREEN PEA SOUP

2 cups dried green peas
2 quarts cold water
⅓ cup chopped celery
1 grated onion
2 tablespoons butter or margarine
1 teaspoon yeast flakes
½ teaspoon salt substitute

Cover peas with water and soak overnight. Cook in same water until tender. Add celery and onion during last hour of cooking. Soup should be thick when done and may be strained, if desired. Add butter, yeast flakes and desired salt substitute just before serving. Serves 4.

CORN CHOWDER

2 cups cooked corn
2 tablespoons butter or margarine
2 minced onions
2 cups diced, raw potatoes
1 teaspoon salt substitute
2 cups boiling water
2 cups milk
½ teaspoon flour blended with 2
    tablespoons water
1 teaspoon yeast flakes

Melt butter in large saucepan. Add onion and brown to golden brown. Add water and potatoes. When potatoes are tender, add corn and milk. Bring to boil. Thicken with flour mixture. Add yeast flakes.

Season according to taste and serve promptly.
Serves 4-6.

HOMEMADE CREAM OF CELERY SOUP

3 stalks chopped celery, including leaves
1 slice onion, chopped
1 cup thin cream
1 cup milk
3 tablespoons flour
3 tablespoons butter or margarine
1 tablespoon yeast flakes
Salt substitute to taste

Add milk to celery and onion and cook for 20 minutes over boiling water. Add butter and flour, which have been cooked together to smooth paste, stirring in slowly. Season. Add cream and heat to boiling point. Now add yeast flakes. Stir. Serve garnished with bits of finely chopped parsley. Serves 4 to 6.

CHAPTER 13

SAUCES AND DRESSINGS

MUSHROOM SAUCE

4 *tablespoons butter or margarine*
3 *tablespoons whole grain flour*
1½ *cups milk*
½ *teaspoon yeast flakes*
1 *small can mushrooms*

Melt butter, stir in flour, add milk, yeast flakes and blend thoroughly. Cook over medium heat about 10 minutes, stirring constantly. Add mushrooms. Serve piping hot. Serves 4 to 6.

CHEESE SAUCE

2 *tablespoons butter or margarine*
1 *tablespoon flour*
1 *cup milk*
½ *teaspoon yeast flakes*
¼ *cup grated cheese*
Salt substitute

Melt butter, add flour and stir to smooth paste.
Add milk, yeast flakes and desired seasoning, mixing well. Cook slowly for 5 minutes, stirring constantly. Add cheese and remove immediately from
stove. Blend thoroughly and serve piping hot. Serves
2 to 4.

OIL DRESSING

1 *cup apple cider vinegar*
¾ *cup vegetable oil*
1 *teaspoon yeast flakes*
½ *cup honey*
1 *teaspoon salt substitute*
1 *teaspoon paprika*
1 *teaspoon celery seed*

Combine all ingredients in bottle or jar. Cover and
shake very well. Keep stored in refrigerator. Always
shake well before serving. Serves 8 to 10.

ROQUEFORT DRESSING

1 *cup vegetable oil*
¼ *lb. Roquefort cheese, mashed*
½ *teaspoon paprika*
½ *tablespoon salt substitute*
½ *teaspoon honey*
½ *teaspoon yeast flakes*
½ *cup lemon juice*

Mix seasonings, honey and yeast flakes. Add olive oil and cheese and beat until smooth. Makes 6 ⅓-cup portions for raw vegetable salads.

HOLLANDAISE SAUCE

½ *cup butter or margarine*
4 *egg yolks, well beaten*
2 *tablespoons lemon juice*
¼ *teaspoon salt substitute*
½ *teaspoon yeast flakes*
Dash of cayenne
¼ *cup boiling water*

Divide butter into two portions. Place one portion in top of double boiler. Add beaten egg yolks and lemon juice and place over hot water (not boiling), stirring constantly until butter is melted. Add all remaining ingredients and continue stirring until this butter also is melted. Add boiling water to mixture and cook, stirring until thick. Remove from heat. Serve over salads. Makes about 2 cups.

CREAMY MINT DRESSING

2 *tablespoons finely chopped fresh mint*
  leaves
1 *teaspoon honey*
1 *teaspoon lemon juice*
½ *teaspoon yeast flakes*
1 *cup sour cream*

Add mint, honey, lemon juice and yeast flakes to sour cream; fold in gently but thoroughly. Blend together. Chill for several hours or overnight before serving. TIP: Delicious when served over fruit salad, tomato slices, meat salad (especially lamb). Makes 1 cup.

CHAPTER 14

DESSERTS

BAKED RICE PUDDING

1 *cup natural brown rice*
1½ *cups milk*
2 *eggs, beaten*
¼ *cup honey*
1 *teaspoon vanilla*
1 *teaspoon yeast flakes*
¼ *cup sun-dried raisins*
Cinnamon

Cook rice according to package directions. Add milk. Boil gently 5 minutes, stirring occasionally. Combine eggs, honey, vanilla, yeast flakes. Slowly stir in rice. Add raisins. Pour into 1½-quart oiled casserole. Sprinkle top with cinnamon. Place in pan containing one-half inch hot water. Bake 35 to 40 minutes in 350°F. oven or until knife inserted near edge comes out clean. Serves 4 to 5.

THREE FRUIT PIE

> 1 cup chopped cranberries
> 1 cup chopped, tart apples
> 1 cup honey
> 1 teaspoon yeast flakes
> ¼ cup drained, crushed pineapple

Combine all ingredients and let stand up to 3 hours. Meanwhile, line a pie pan with pastry. Now add the filling and cover with a top crust, sealing the edges carefully. Bake for 10 minutes in a hot oven at 400°F. Then reduce heat and bake for 40 minutes in a moderate oven at 350°F. Serves 4 to 6.

LEMON DAINTY PUDDING

> 3 tablespoons vegetable oil
> 1 teaspoon yeast flakes
> ¾ cup honey
> 2 tablespoons flour
> 2 eggs, separated
> 1 cup milk
> Juice and grated rind of 1 lemon

Combine oil with yeast flakes and honey. Now add flour and blend until smooth and creamy. Add beaten egg yolks, milk, lemon juice and rind. Beat mixture until light and smooth. Fold in stiffly beaten egg whites. Place in oiled baking dish set in pan of hot water. Bake in moderate oven at 350°F. until pudding is delicate brown. Pudding should be tender sponge on top, with golden-yellow sauce underneath. Pudding may be baked in individual molds, if desired. Serves 4 to 6.

LEMON SHERBET

6 tablespoons lemon juice
2 tablespoons orange juice
1 cup honey
2 egg whites, stiffly beaten
½ cup cream, whipped
1 teaspoon yeast flakes
¾ cup water

Combine honey and water and boil for 10 minutes. Remove from heat and cool. Now mix together fruit juices with yeast flakes. Add to honey-water syrup. Fold in egg whites and whipped cream. Let cool. Now pour into refrigerator tray and place in freezer until firm. Serves 4 to 6.

BAKED CUSTARD

3 eggs
⅓ cup honey
1 teaspoon yeast flakes
3 cups milk, scalded
1 teaspoon vanilla

Beat eggs slightly. Add honey and yeast flakes. Mix well. Add milk gradually, stirring vigorously. Add vanilla. Pour into custard cups. Now place cups in baking pan; pour boiling water around them to almost the height of the custard. Bake in a moderate oven, 350°F., 30 to 35 minutes or until a silver knife inserted in the custard comes out clean. Remove cups from water; cool on rack. Chill thoroughly. Serve in cups or loosen around edge with paring knife, then turn out. Serves 6.

HONEY FLAVORED WALNUTS

1 cup honey
½ cup sour cream
1 teaspoon vanilla
1 teaspoon yeast flakes
2½ cups walnut halves

Bring honey and sour cream to a boil in heavy saucepan, stirring constantly. Cook to soft-ball stage, 236°F. to 238°F. Now remove from heat. Add vanilla, yeast flakes; beat until mixture begins to thicken. Add nuts. Stir until well coated. Turn out on greased cookie sheet; separate in individual serving pieces. Makes about 1 pound of honey flavored walnuts.

ORANGE TAPIOCA

6 cups orange juice
2 tablespoons lime juice
¼ cup honey
6 tablespoons tapioca
6 thin slices lime
6 teaspoons sour cream
1 teaspoon yeast flakes
Ground cinnamon

Combine orange juice, lime juice, honey, tapioca in a saucepan. Bring to a boil over medium heat, stirring mixture constantly. Remove from heat. Cool, stirring in the yeast flakes. Chill. To serve, spoon into dessert dishes and garnish each portion with a slice of lime topped with 1 teaspoon of sour cream and a dash of cinnamon. Serves 6.

INDEX